A Bath for Steph

By Sally Cowan

This is my dog, Steph.

When we go for a long walk, she jumps in the muck!

Mum gets some things from the shed.

Steph has to get in this big bath tub.

"Quick, Steph!
Get in the bath!" I tell her.

But Steph is not in a rush
to get in!

Steph is such a big dog!

I wet her with Mum.

I check that Steph is all wet.

Then I rub thick suds into the fuzz on her neck and back.

Mum can get the thick suds off Steph.

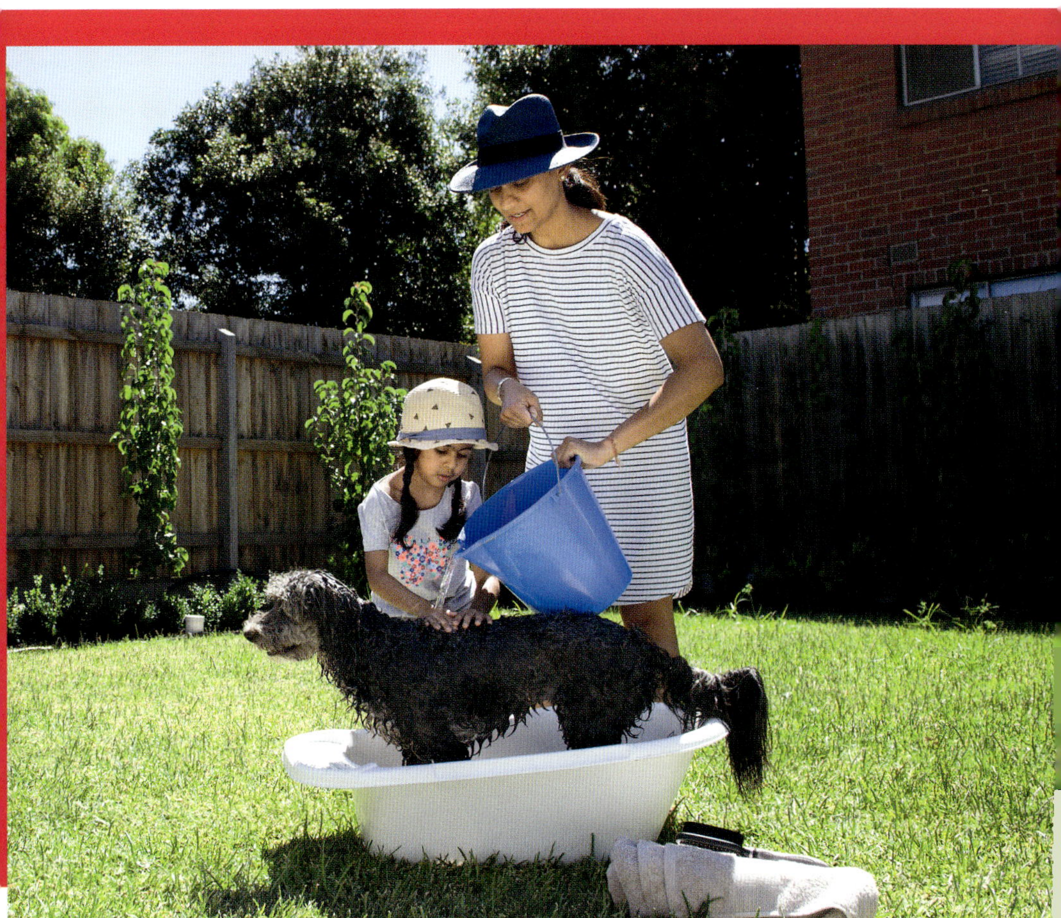

Then I rub Steph with a cloth as I chat with her.

She loves it!

Mum puts the bath things back in the shed.

I sit with Steph.

What a chill dog!

CHECKING FOR MEANING

1. Where does the girl rub the suds on Steph? *(Literal)*
2. Who gets the suds off Steph? *(Literal)*
3. Does Steph like getting in the bath tub? How do you know? *(Inferential)*

EXTENDING VOCABULARY

muck	What is muck? What kind of muck might Steph have rolled in?
shed	What is a shed? What things might you keep in a shed?
chat	What is another word for *chat*?

MOVING BEYOND THE TEXT

1. What are the steps you should follow when you wash an animal, such as a dog?
2. What steps should you follow when you wash your hands?
3. Steph had a bath on a sunny day. Do you think it is better to wash an animal in warm weather or cold weather? Why?
4. What other things might the girl do to take care of Steph?

SPEED SOUNDS

PRACTICE WORDS

Steph

when

this

long

muck

the

things

she

quick

bath

check

rush

such

with

thick

cloth

chill

shed

then

that

what

neck

back

chat